# Here Comes the Taxman!

## British Taxes on American Colonies

Grade 7 Children's American History

**BABY PROFESSOR**
EDUCATION KIDS

First Edition, 2022

Published in the United States by Speedy Publishing LLC, 40 E Main Street, Newark, Delaware 19711 USA.

© 2022 Baby Professor Books, an imprint of Speedy Publishing LLC

Baby Professor Books are available at special discounts when purchased in bulk for industrial and sales-promotional use. For details contact our Special Sales Team at Speedy Publishing LLC, 40 E Main Street, Newark, Delaware 19711 USA. Telephone (888) 248-4521 Fax: (210) 519-4043.

10 9 8 7 6 * 5 4 3 2 1

Print Edition: 9781541955547
Digital Edition: 9781541958548
Hardcover Edition: 9781541996922

See the world in pictures. Build your knowledge in style.
www.speedypublishing.com

# Table of Contents

Do you think that the government has the right to increase taxes?

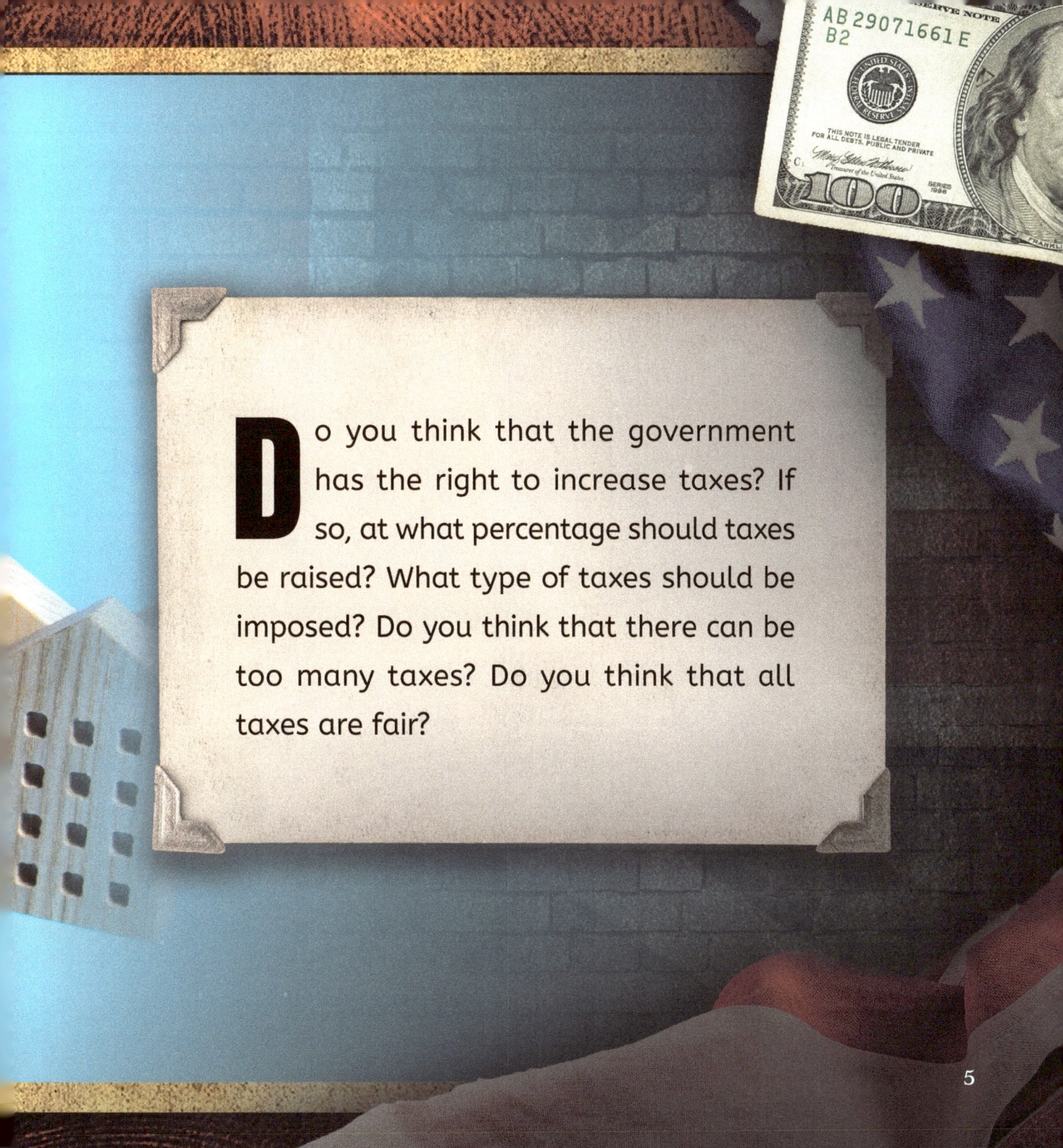

Do you think that the government has the right to increase taxes? If so, at what percentage should taxes be raised? What type of taxes should be imposed? Do you think that there can be too many taxes? Do you think that all taxes are fair?

In the 17th Century, England had control of colonies in North America. To make money, England decided to place different taxes on the colonies. This book will discuss these taxes. The first chapter will give a brief background to the main reason for taxes. The second chapter will focus on different acts that the England enforced. The third chapter will discuss the effects of these acts. It will also show how England responded to these effects.

To make money, England decided to place different taxes on the colonies.

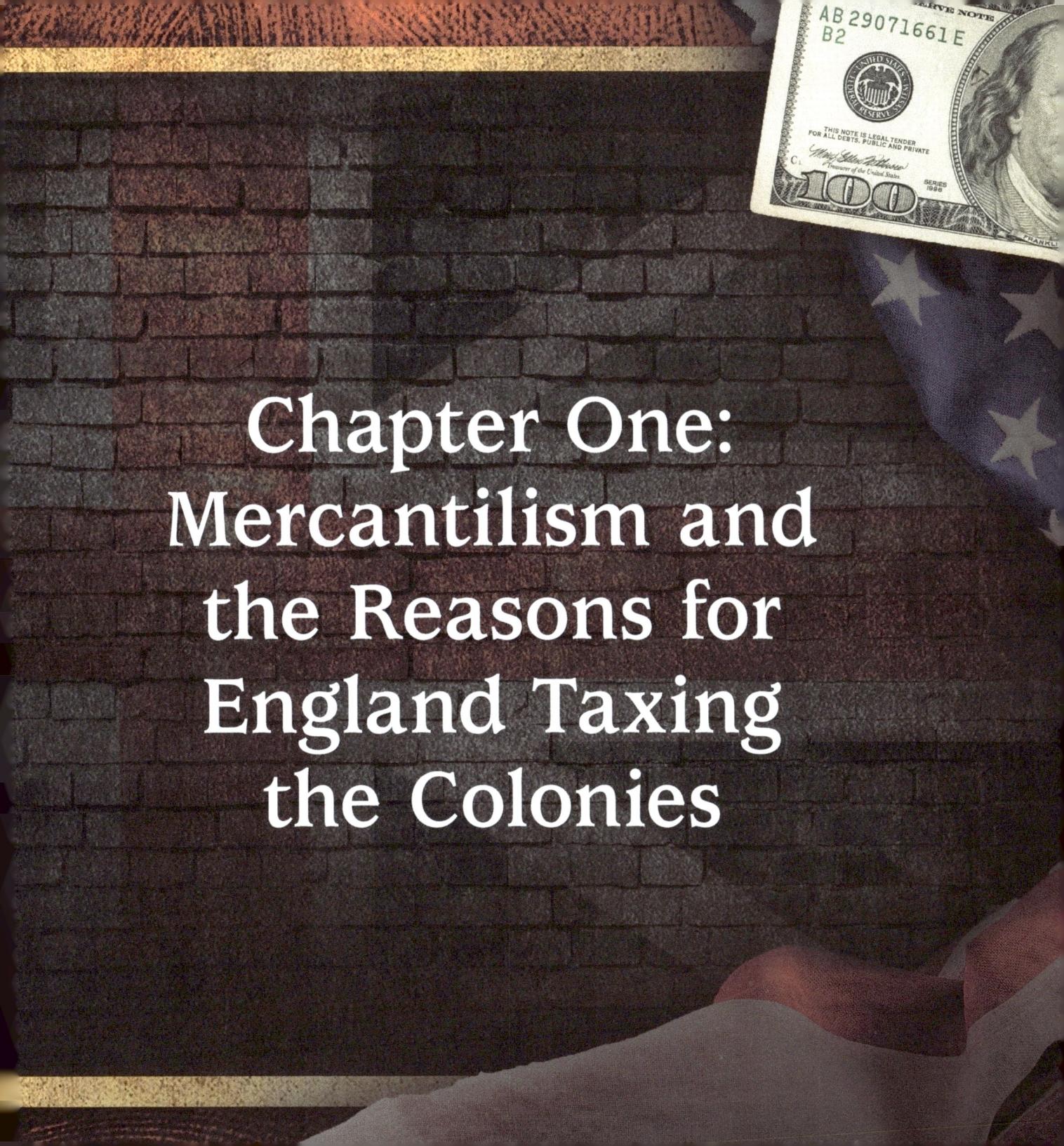

# Chapter One: Mercantilism and the Reasons for England Taxing the Colonies

In the 17th Century, the English government had certain aims. One was to manage all goods that were imported and exported. The goal was to have fewer goods imported than those which were being exported.

In the 17th century, the English government aimed to manage all imported and exported goods.

Another aim was to refuse entry of foreign vessels into England and the English colonies.

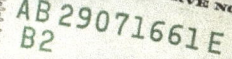

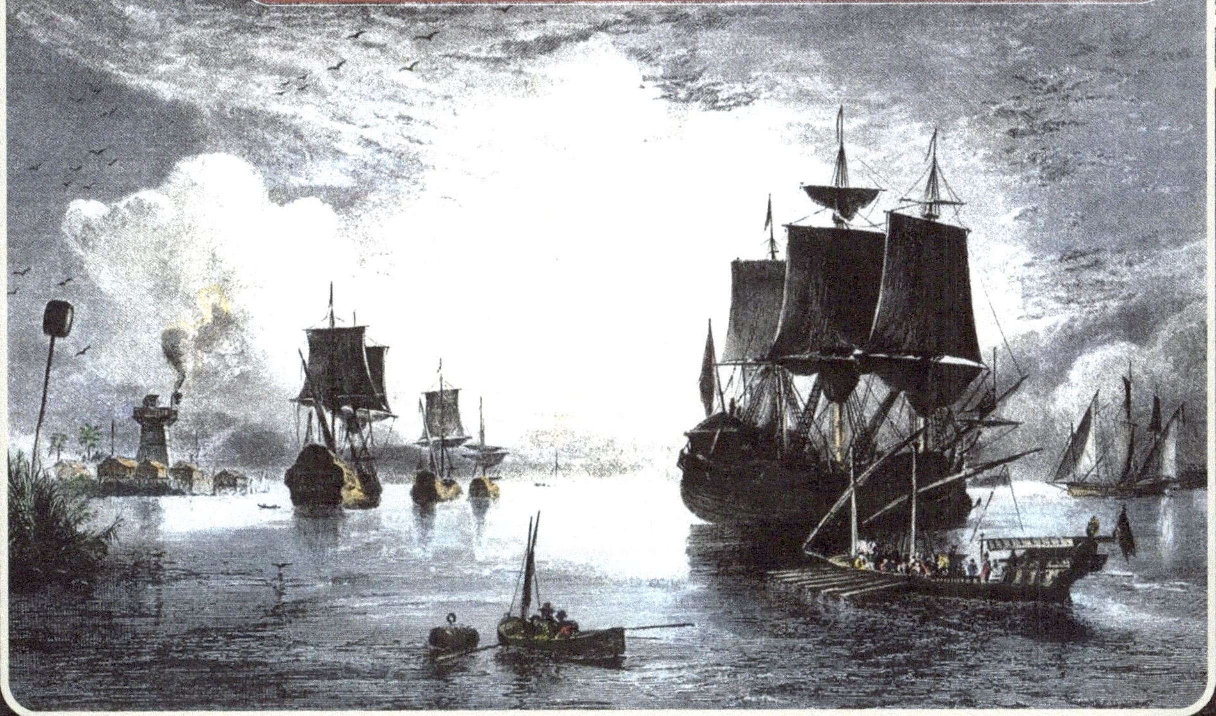

By doing so, it was expected that manufacturing companies and merchants in England would benefit financially. Another aim was to control the economy in the colonies. A third was to refuse entry of foreign vessels into England and the English colonies.

There were a couple major reasons for these aims. One was an idea or theory known as mercantilism. It was a theory of economics that became popular during the 16th Century. It had several principles. If a country were to follow these principles, it could expect its economy to flourish.

If a country were to follow the principles of mercantilism,
it could expect its economy to flourish.

13

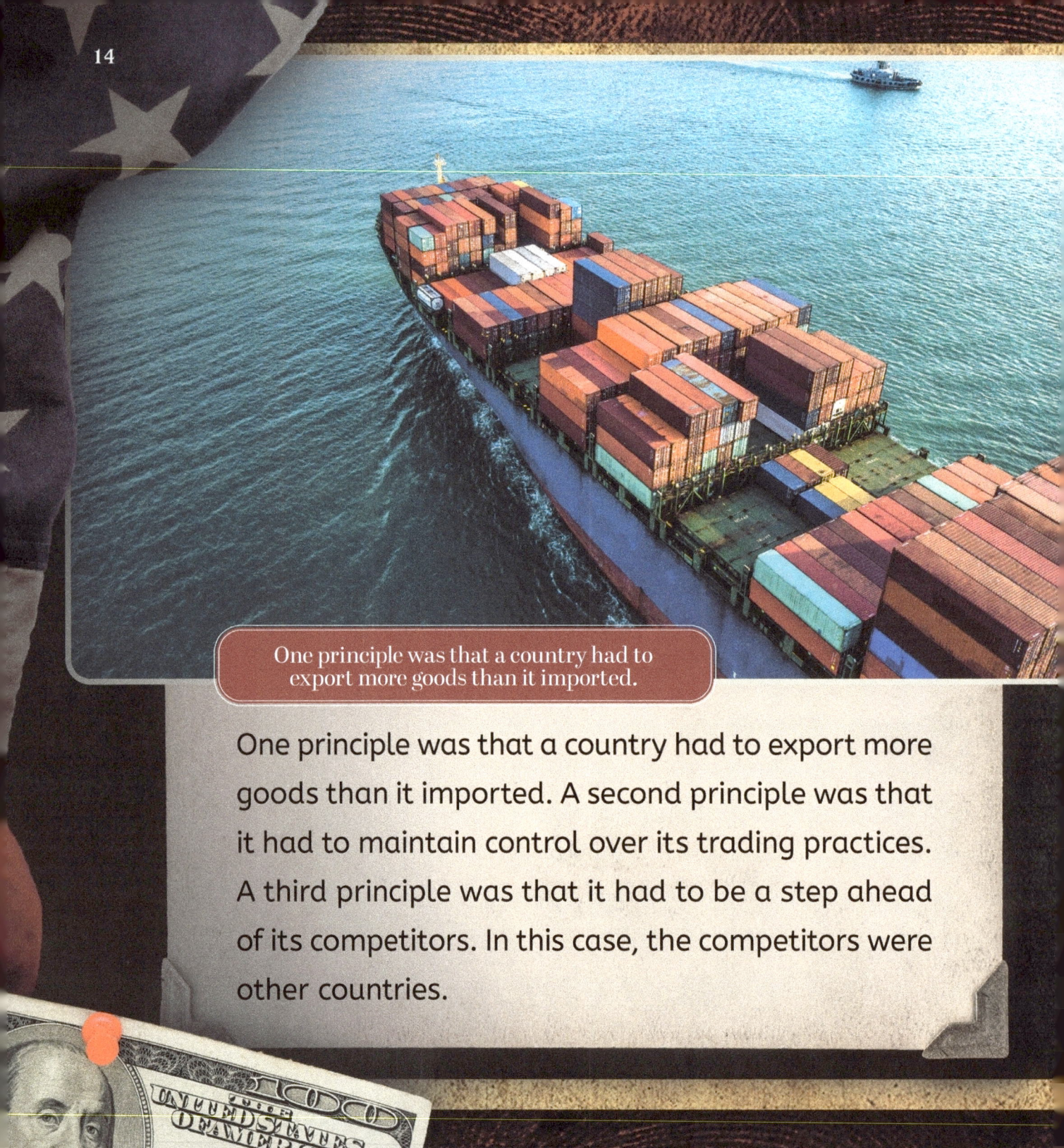

One principle was that a country had to export more goods than it imported.

One principle was that a country had to export more goods than it imported. A second principle was that it had to maintain control over its trading practices. A third principle was that it had to be a step ahead of its competitors. In this case, the competitors were other countries.

A fourth principle was that it should keep valuable metals like gold and silver within its borders. The final principle was that it had to set up many colonies. By doing so, it would always have natural resources along with products.

Another principle was that it should keep valuable metals like gold and silver within its borders.

Another reason was what was happening politically in England. At this time, Oliver Cromwell and the English Parliament ruled England and the English colonies. England had just come out of a Civil War in which the king was beheaded.

The execution of King Charles I of England

Oliver Cromwell making his first speech in Parliament.

Oliver Cromwell

The new leader was Oliver Cromwell who held the title of Lord Protector of England, Scotland, and Ireland. Both Cromwell and the English Parliament wanted to keep themselves in power. They were also in need of <u>revenue</u>.

There was one major hindrance to Cromwell and the English Parliament achieving their plan. The Netherlands was the country that had control of international trade. In addition, the Dutch had amazing vessels known as flyboats or fluits. These vessels transported many types of goods at low prices. They were also reliable.

Model of a Dutch fluit, a 16th century sailing ship designed for cheap and efficient transoceanic delivery.

An illustration of Hudson's vessel, The Halve Maen or Half Moon, when it was first discovered in the Hudson River.

# Did you know?

Other countries started to use the fluit. England was one. The fluit typically had two masts, a topsail, and a main sail. The explorer Henry Hudson used a fluit in the early 1600s. He set sail many times to try to find the Northwest Passage. The fluit was often used in the trade industry during this time.

Henry Hudson

Cromwell and the English Parliament were upset that they could not compete with the Dutch.

Cromwell and the English Parliament were upset that they had colonies, yet they could not compete with the Dutch. Their reason for having colonies was for power and wealth. To do something to <u>impede</u> the Dutch's grip on trade, Cromwell and the English Parliament came up with different acts.

Cromwell ended up disbanding Parliament in 1653. He died five years later. In less than two years, the English monarchy returned to power.

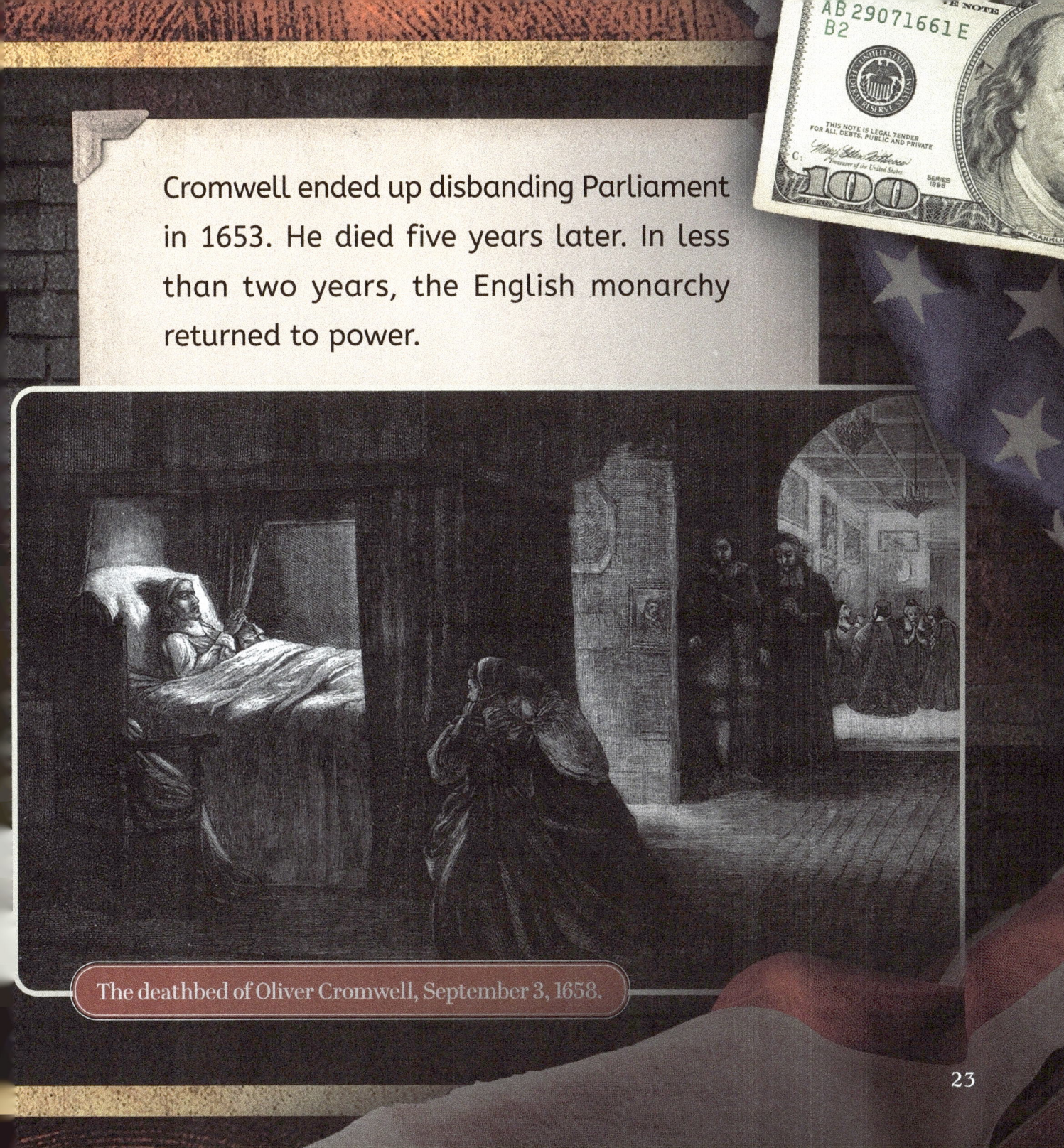

The deathbed of Oliver Cromwell, September 3, 1658.

# Chapter Two:
# The Navigation Acts, The Wool Act, The Molasses Act, The Hat Act, The Iron Act, The Stamp Act, The Townshend Acts, and The Tea Act

All products being imported to England and any English colony had to be transported in English ships.

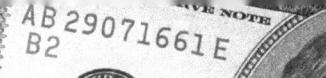

# The Navigation Acts:

The Navigation Acts were approved in October 1651. There were several requirements. All products being imported to England and any English colony had to be transported in English ships. This applied to products that came from Africa, Asia and parts of North America that were not controlled by England. If products were coming from European countries, they too had to be transported in English ships. If the products originated in a different country, they had to be shipped directly from the country of origin.

There were specific requirements for marine products. Only English vessels could catch whales, herring, cod, and any other type of fish. This was extended to products that were made from whales and other fish. An example would be fish oil.

Only English vessels could catch whales, herring, cod, and any other type of fish.

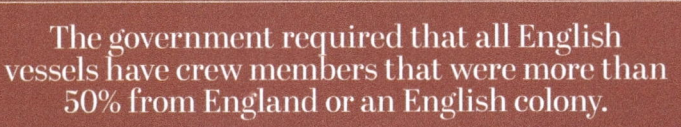
The government required that all English vessels have crew members that were more than 50% from England or an English colony.

The English had their own criteria for what qualified as an English vessel. It was one whose owner was from England. The government also required that all English vessels have crew members that were more than fifty percent from England or an English colony.

Some of the requirements had a significant impact on the thirteen colonies in North America. Before a ship could transport products to the American colonies, it was required to go to England. There, it would be taxed on the products before they were allowed to continue to North America. This was called an import duty. Naturally, this drove the price of the products up by the time the colonists could buy them.

Import duty is a tax collected on imports by a country's customs authorities.

Steam-driven boat loading bales of cotton at a plantation pier.

Some goods were classified as enumerated articles. These were goods that were needed in England but were unable to be made there. At first some of these goods were cotton, rice, and tobacco. Later, furs, sugar, indigo, and shipbuilding materials were added.

A lot of colonists were upset about these requirements. They were forced to sell products to the English when they could have made more money by selling them elsewhere. There were certain goods that the colonists could sell to other countries. Examples were wheat and fish. This was only because the English were able to produce these goods themselves.

Colonists farming wheat along the Delaware River in New Sweden, 1600s.

Colonists drying and salting fish on the Atlantic shore.

# The Wool Act:

This act forbade American colonists from exporting any product that was made from wool. It was passed in 1699.

Patriotic American colonial woman spinning to avoid importing British cloth.

Colourful dyed strands of wool for weaving clothes in spinning mill.

In 1707, Scotland merged with England to form one country. It was Britain.

The Scottish Duke of Queensbury presenting to Queen Anne of England the Act of Union, creating Great Britain in 1707.

The rum merchants were forced to purchase molasses from the British West Indies.

## The Molasses Act:

This act hurt the rum merchants in the New England colonies. It was passed in 1733. They were forced to purchase molasses from the British West Indies. Although the Dutch and French also sold this product, the colonists could not buy from them.

# The Hat Act:

This act forbade the colonists to export any hats that were made from beaver fur. It was passed in 1732.

The Hat Act forbade the colonists to export any hats that were made from beaver fur.

# Did you know?

The American beaver lives in the woods of North America. It builds its home, called a dam, in a stream. At one time, the fur trade was common in North America. Its fur was highly sought after. Beaver fur was the number one trading item in the area Oregon. The *Beaver State* is a nickname for Oregon.

A North American beaver working on its dam.

The Iron Act forbade the colonists to make goods from iron.

## The Iron Act:

This act forbade the colonists to make goods from iron. This meant that they could not manufacture hardware, utensils, or tools. It was passed in 1750.

# The Stamp Act:

The Stamp Act became law in 1765. It required all colonists in North America to buy stamps from Britain. The stamps were used on any legal document. Examples included marriage licenses, wills, and land deeds. Other items which required the stamp were newspapers, playing cards, dice, almanacs, and pamphlets.

British soldiers enforcing the Stamp Act.

# The Townshend Acts:

The Townshend Acts came into effect in 1767. They contained four separate laws. The first act was directly aimed at the New York Assembly. It was to punish the assembly for refusing to pay the costs of keeping British soldiers in New York. The costs included paying for housing, transporting, and feeding the soldiers. The assembly was put on suspension until it covered these costs.

The first law was to punish the assembly for refusing to pay the costs of keeping British soldiers in New York.

The costs included paying for housing, transporting, and feeding the soldiers.

The second law put a tax on several items that the colonists would purchase.

The second law put a tax on several items that the colonists would purchase. These items were tea, paint, paper, lead, and glass.

The third law dealt with how the taxes would be collected.

The fourth law took away the costs that the British tea merchants had to pay to ship their tea to the colonists.

# The Tea Act:

The Tea Act came into effect in 1773. It put all the selling and delivering of tea into the hands of one company. The company was called the East India Tea Company. This meant that the colonists could only get its tea from this company. To make matters worse, there was a tax added to the tea. At the time, tea was the beverage which most colonists drank.

Unloading tea ships in the British East India Company docks in London.

THE TEA ACT OF 1773 is read out at a meeting in Faneuil Hall.

> Nothing was thought of but this taxation,
> and the easiest method of liquidation.
>
> # T-A-X
>
> 'Twas enough to vex
> the souls of the men of Boston town,
> to read this under the seal of the crown.
>
> TAX ON TEA.
> 3d per lb
>
> They were loyal subjects of George the third,
> So they believed and so they averred,
> But this bristling, offensive placard set
> on the walls, was worse than a bayonet.

Colonists learn of the Tea Act of 1773.

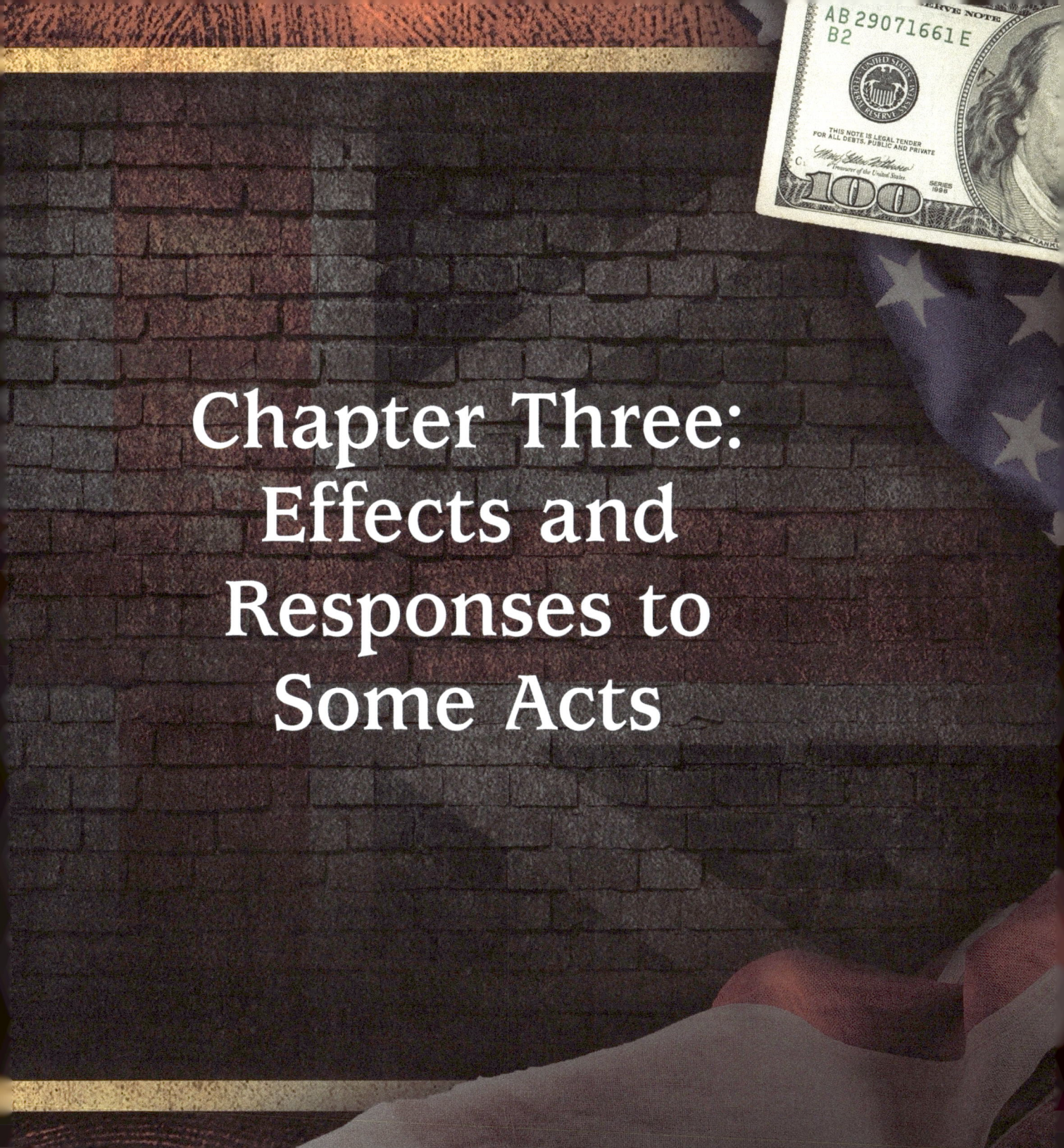

# Chapter Three: Effects and Responses to Some Acts

The Navigation Acts ended up causing the First Anglo-Dutch War. This war started in 1652 and ended two years later. The Dutch were upset because they were being prevented from taking part in trade with England and the colonies.

Battle of Scheveningen, Naval battle near Ter Heijde on August 10, 1653, during the First Anglo-Dutch War.

Protest in New York City by colonists opposing the Stamp Act 1765.

Several people who were directly affected by the Stamp Act voiced their opposition. These were clergy, lawyers, newspaper editors, and printers.

Sons of Liberty protesting the Stamp Act by attacking the house of Lieutenant Governor Thomas Hutchinson in Boston on August 26, 1765.

Some colonists began to come up with societies to protest. One example was the Sons and Daughters of Liberty. These people organized ways to stand up against what they thought was unfair. They boycotted products, for instance.

Britain responded by repealing the Stamp Act. However, the Declaratory Act was issued. It said that Britain was within its right to enforce taxes in the colonies.

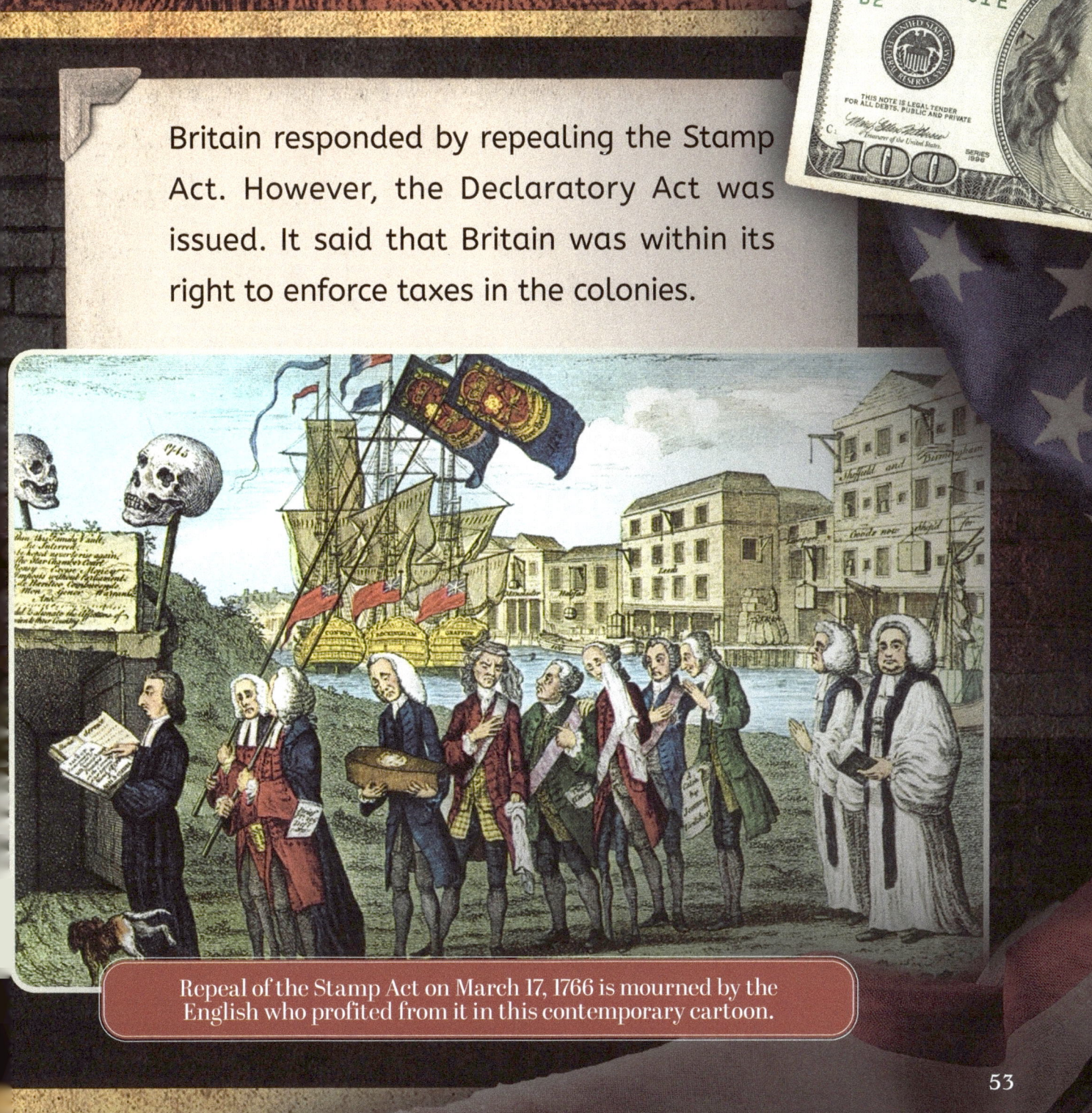

Repeal of the Stamp Act on March 17, 1766 is mourned by the English who profited from it in this contemporary cartoon.

Many people vowed to never obey the Townshend Acts. There were some violent protests. Another form of opposition to the Townshend Acts was the Massachusetts Circular Letter. The Massachusetts House of Representatives was responsible for it. It officially rejected the taxes.

Britain responded by repealing all the Townshend Acts except taxing tea.

Many people vowed to never obey the Townshend Acts.

There were some violent protests.

Colonists throwing boxes of tea overboard during the Boston Tea Party, 1773.

Having to pay taxes on tea and only going through the East India Tea Company greatly upset many colonists. They showed their <u>contempt</u> by throwing out all the tea that arrived in Boston Harbor. It happened on December 16, 1773. This event is known as the Boston Tea Party.

The British Parliament responded by coming up with the Coercive Acts. They are also known as the Intolerable Acts. There were five acts in total.

A colonial American cartoon depicting how the Intolerable Acts are affecting the colonists, the British Parliament and King George III.

A VIEW OF THE TOWN OF BOSTON WITH SEVERAL SHIPS OF WAR IN THE HARBOUR

In an attempt to control the angry colonists, Britain sent its warships to Boston in 1774.

One was the Boston Port Act. It required Boston harbor to be closed until the total cost of the tea was paid. This was the tea that had been ruined during the Boston Tea Party.

British soldiers quartered in an American colonial home, 1770s.

The Massachusetts Government Act was another act. The British forced the local council of Massachusetts to lose their role. A new council was appointed. Another was the Administration of Justice Act. This act gave the new governor the authority to allow British officers to be tried elsewhere. The Quartering Act was another act. It gave British soldiers the permission to stay in people's homes.

The final act was the Quebec Act. It allowed the Canadian province of Quebec power over territory in the Ohio valley.

Quebec Act 1774

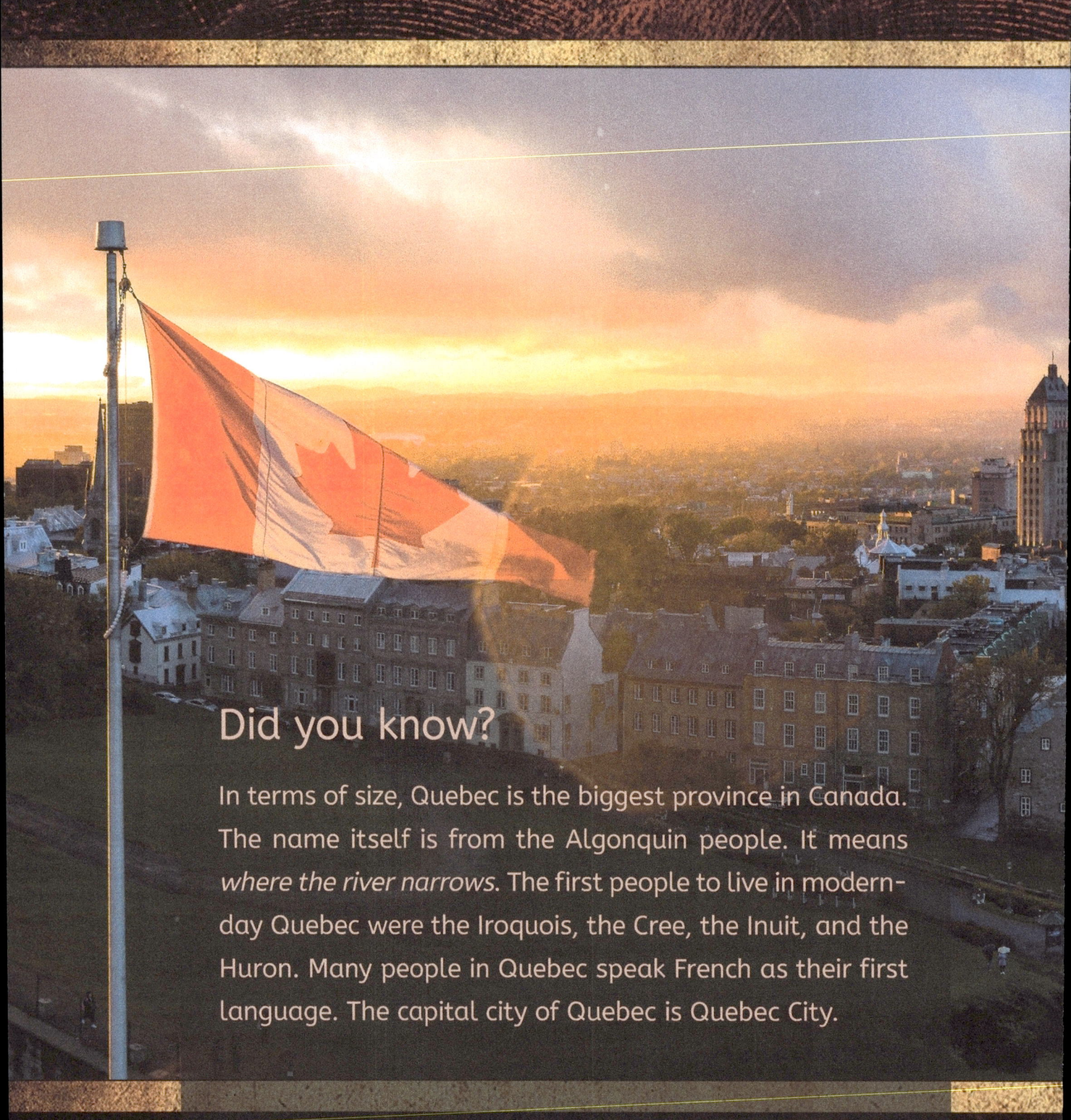

## Did you know?

In terms of size, Quebec is the biggest province in Canada. The name itself is from the Algonquin people. It means *where the river narrows*. The first people to live in modern-day Quebec were the Iroquois, the Cree, the Inuit, and the Huron. Many people in Quebec speak French as their first language. The capital city of Quebec is Quebec City.

Quebec, Canada.

Over time, the colonists would end up rebelling against England. They would eventually declare their independence. The American Revolution War would be fought. The thirteen colonies would form their own country.

Over time, the colonists would end up rebelling against England.

The Declaration of Independence, July 4, 1776.

# Summary

By following the principles of mercantilism and in an effort to gain wealth, England passed several acts. Many of these acts were not well received. The Dutch as well as the colonists in North America were upset. This is because many of the acts affected them negatively. The colonists started to express their anger at many of the acts.

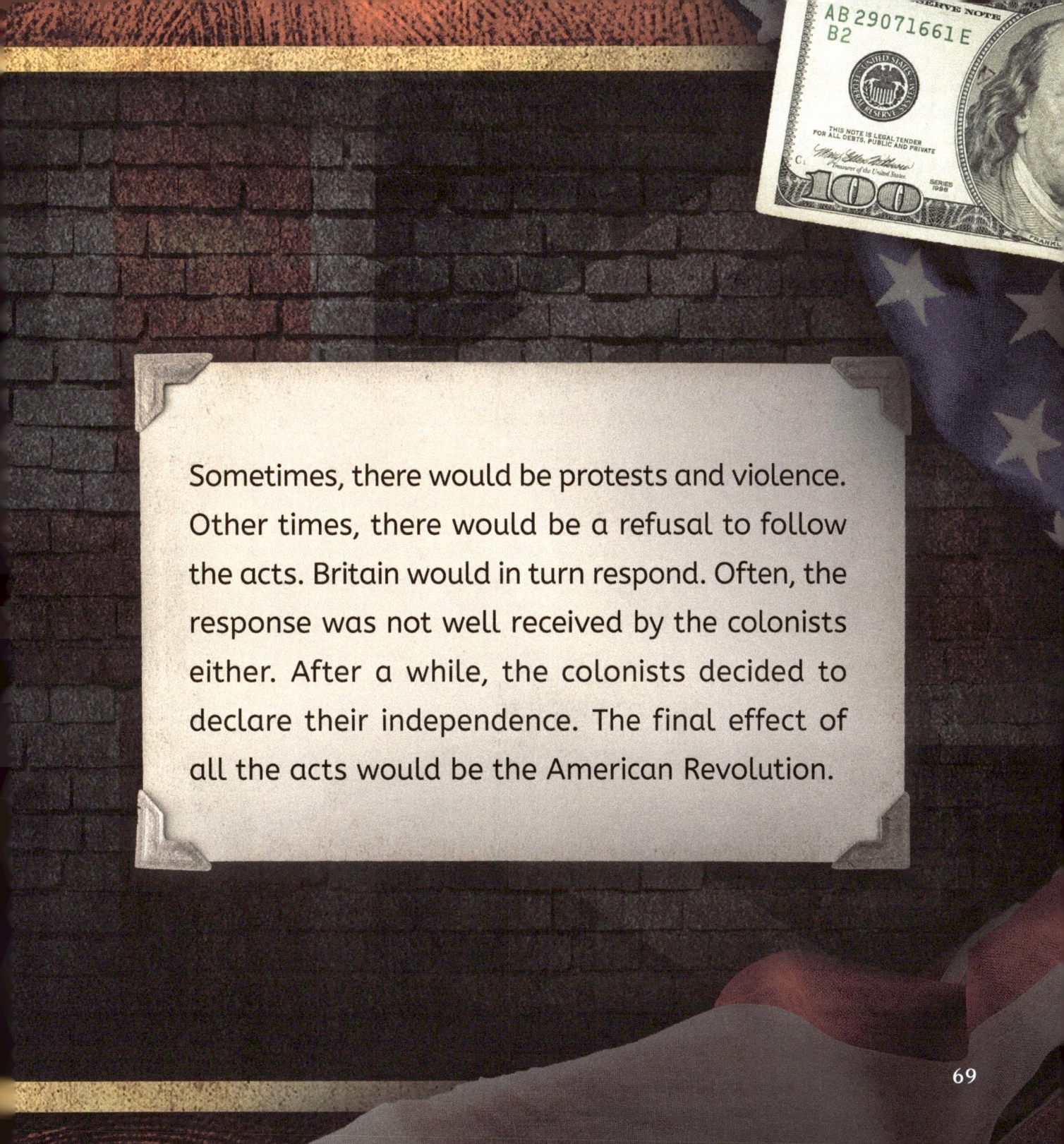

Sometimes, there would be protests and violence. Other times, there would be a refusal to follow the acts. Britain would in turn respond. Often, the response was not well received by the colonists either. After a while, the colonists decided to declare their independence. The final effect of all the acts would be the American Revolution.

# Glossary

Revenue (pg. 17): money, especially that which a company or organization receives

Impede (pg. 22): delay, prevent, or hinder

Contempt (pg. 57): a strong feeling of disrespect and/or dislike

*Visit*

## www.speedypublishing.com

To view and download free content on your
favorite subject and browse our catalog of new
and exciting books for readers of all ages.

Printed in the USA
CPSIA information can be obtained
at www.ICGtesting.com
JSHW071903250924
70364JS00002B/2